darkacre

darkacre

POEMS

Greg Hewett

COFFEE HOUSE PRESS

MINNEAPOLIS

2010

Coffee House Press books are available to the trade through our primary distributor, Consortium Book Sales & Distribution, www.cbsd.com or (800) 283-3572. For personal orders, catalogs, or other information, write to: info@coffeehousepress.org.

Coffee House Press is a nonprofit literary publishing house. Support from private foundations, corporate giving programs, government programs, and generous individuals helps make the publication of our books possible. We gratefully acknowledge their support in detail in the back of this book.

Good books are brewing at coffeehousepress.org

LIBRARY OF CONGRESS CATALOGING-IN-PUBLICATION DATA
Hewett, Greg.
Darkacre : poetry / by Greg Hewett.
p. cm.
ISBN 978-1-56689-245-2 (alk. paper)
I. Title.
PS3558.E826D37 2010
811'.54—DC22
2009051518

PRINTED IN THE UNITED STATES
1 3 5 7 9 8 6 4 2
FIRST EDITION | FIRST PRINTING | APRIL 2010

ACKNOWLEDGMENTS
Earlier versions of "Island," "Lapidary," "elements," "seeing," "five appearances," and "bound" were first published in the following artist books from Strong Silent Type Press, images and design by Fred Hagstrom: *Bound* (2004), *Junked* (2005), *First Light* (2005), *Echo* (2007), *His Small Self Constant, Variable* (2008).

My gratitude to Fred Hagstrom for asking me to collaborate on his profoundly beautiful book-art. Thanks to my brother, Harold Hewett, for the tutorial on property law and real property rights, with all the great terminology such as blackacre, faggot of rights, and fertile octogenarian. To Chris Fischbach, Allan Kornblum, Molly Mikolowski, Linda Koutsky, and the rest of the team at Coffee House Press, I want to express my continued admiration for the work you do and thank you for once again standing by my work. And Ted Mathys, what would I do without you turning your eye once again toward my poetry?

This book is for Tony Hainault,
who has taught me how
to see the land beyond darkacre.

darkacre

real property rights

to assert the alienable right
to use and abuse the corporeal
hereditaments
common law offers owner a faggot under condition
one stick be given away
for the incorporeal
hereditaments such as
easement (e.g. widening freeway; extension of easy street)
or floating easement (e.g. access for utility workers; ingress and egress for
  artist with easel seeking the inaccessible, the sublime)
one stick for zoning (e.g. removal of colossus of love in blue neon above
  gable in residential)
one stick for nuisance (e.g. hounds of hell baying all night from owner's backyard)
one stick for national defense (e.g. billeting of soldiers; grassy graves for the fallen)
one stick for airspace (e.g. jets; ghosts on aerial waves)
one stick for the space-time imperative (without which we could not perceive property,
  let alone boundary, landscape, or land)
one stick for the categories of imagination (without which there is nothing of this earth
  and nothing beyond)
this faggot of rights because what is of one may not be of the other
and thus the tragedy of the commons

darkacre

dominion granted over darkacre
in perpetuity   measured
from the northeast corner
of the deconsecrated church past
memory   to the ancient
oak somehow immune
from hewing at the northwest
to the limit of the decommissioned
reactor to the southwest
to the ruins of the capitol
of empire lost
to the southeast   and not
from the river (for that changes with rain, with flood)
and not from the coast (for that changes with every tide)
and including airspace
straight up to the heavens
with stars for metes and bounds
and straight down to the heavens'
opposite   to the molten core
        dominion granted in perpetuity for as long as
        a fertile octogenarian can pass it on

blackacre

darkacre grants owner of blackacre covenant
over grand onyx lobbies
plazas   esplanades   et cetera
in addition to soil sealed beneath their polished slabs   so rich
            peas and beans once yielded abundantly there
and including subsurface rights
to slaves in unmarked graves
            owner must however
allow continuance
of right of way for subterranean
railway and equitable servitude
of one man under no nation
who cleans the third rail without fear
of violet electrocution
at overtime rate
singing a nocturne with no moon
dreaming of a lost island
his dark eyes reflecting ultramarine

whiteacre

darkacre conveys deed to whiteacre
at the boundary where snow falls
(or is it petals? ash?) slowly down
to mix with sand drifting   sifting
in wind   in perpetual
glare   the only clear feature
a vast flock of translucent
shopping bags   each tethered
to a dried stalk of chicory

grayacre

darkacre repeals statute of limitations
on language for grayacre
      site of the marketplace of
everything under the sun
and pluto   thereby providing another
way of speaking in said
marketplace   not so black and white
     a spectral way   a parallel way   for example
a whale swallowing a man
or ramming a ship
or just being a damn leviathan
can make many things
manifest   such as destiny
obedience   human nature
     or on homelier terms
who is more guilty
a man who steals a goose
from the commons or the other
who steals the commons
from under the goose
or from a goose-eye view
the one who steals the whole
ocean surrounding the whale
who peals nuanced sonar over longitudes
who came to language some
15 million years before we ever kenned
whale-road   and made all gory
in the process
     in the abstract grayacre constitutes

the all   agora
in which we speak   and may well be
the ocean too

brownacre

darkacre cedes to brownacre stewardship
of monarchs teetering
on milkweed   of buckthorn
growing amid the fallen
factory in the shape of a basilica
(and dropping berries that stain
cracked concrete and brick indigo)
   of coyotes roaming the dead shopping mall
   of puddles and ponds
   of fires flaring yellow and turquoise
   billowing blackest smoke
where boys melt
plastic in order to smelt
precious metals as they
regard the men at the perimeter
suspiciously

greenacre

darkacre transfers pertinent rights over to greenacre
for construction of paradise
including the right to eradicate
clover and all
broadleaf plants
tendrils   vines   et cetera
native   invasive   or otherwise
deemed by charter unauthorized
while granting airspace to escaped parrots
(insofar as they connote freedom)   at least
before the snow begins
to collect like muslin
on their wings
at which point seasonal variance
for importation and keeping of penguins
granted

redacre

darkacre dedicates redacre to the history
of the brotherhood who lived in silence
raising chickens
men obsessed with the blood
of salvation   who slept on
straw mats in a humble cabin
as vandals of a different kind
of fraternity launched roman
candles from the dark surrounding slopes
laughing through beer   through bright red air
as hens flew low on fire
into the woods and caught the woods
like a dry faggot on fire
and sparks fell onto shingles
over the brothers dreaming of these rebels

darkacre codicil

one who remains   one who collects
the remainder of what was
of another
hereby known as remainderman
has testamentary trust over darkacre
forthwith abrogated
the law being no less
simple than sacrifice
than burying   blood   ash   bone
with golden sheaves and honeycombs
with jars of wine and prayer scrolls
at the termini   in other words
a ritual too simple
to reckon darkacre
        for every subject of property
        may be intangible
and to walk the limits
in the shadowless noon
of virtue is the ultimate purpose
        it is a poem without lines
        it is measuring the border
between this world and possibility
between science and metaphysics
between reason and hope
        for everyman's a remainderman
every boundary evidence
every terminus implication
and every acre dark

Under Auspices

Tornado Edifice

It's the order of things.
Steel cables fray then snap,
Concrete caves in and I-beams collapse.

Wreckage literal as cable news.
In the storm shelters of our hearts
(we sometimes see as catacombs),

Even greater chaos echoes.
Anxiety has become pro forma.
Arcs of desire routinely crumble.

No martyr's aureole is ever awarded
So we opt for halos
around halogen lights.

We contemplate a bird
Once called an oriole
Mimicking a small miracle.

The bird, or the memory
Of the bird, revolves upward
Through shattered vaulting,

Flaming against ozone,
Cracking space open
On its small sharp wing.

In this place without perspective,

In a capsule of ruins
Scorched by our own electric

Thoughts, we inscribe a future:
to live here we will have to re-invent ourselves
to leave here we will have to re-invent ourselves

Cataclysm Edifice

It's the order of things.
Behind the eye, behind the sunlit sky,
A comet moves like clockwork

Toward us, red against the lit
Black of outer space.
This clear oblivion

Will pass unnoticed
Like every other.
Under a tapestry of flowers

Lie fragments of a city,
Each no bigger than
A diamond, a knucklebone.

A girl wearing a chaplet of weeds
In a chapel of cinderblock
Swallows her warning.

A finch the color of salvation
Feeds on thistle beside a stream
That becomes a river, a gulf,

Where a pelican dead
Reckons the coming storm's
Landfall far ahead

Of computer model,

And at the eyewall,
Against sky now violent violet

And pierced by oil platforms,
Pierces its own breast, so,
We believe, that we may be saved.

Riot Edifice

It's the order of things.
A phalanx of police arouses
A flock of pigeons into a helix

Rising iridescent and encoded
Against the incandescent sky.
The birds vanish as transparent

Shields break the crowd apart.
The squad re-forms as circle
Around a solitary boy

The world now centers on, the one
Who refuses to run,
The one who leaps into the air

Like a martial artist,
Nailing a 720 Butterfly Twist,
Kicking every shield twice:

Once for rage, once for liberty.
We want to choreograph our own doom,
And in our falling revive

Something more abstract than the concrete
We land on, something erected
Not in marble, not inscribed.

We want the code of everything revealed

In the flight of pigeons
To cliffs on a faraway coast

Where they return as rock doves,
In bruises the color of their throats
Blooming over our body.

The Structures of Crisis

Stadium Revelation

In the structure of crisis
the world loses scale and you
find your self within yourself
at the bottom of a stadium
deep and lit to reveal
more than sunlight ever could.
Contest over, you stalk
the track, staring up
past metal halides lights into night-
wind hard and directionless.
Banners writhe like dragons.
Kneeling down beneath a galaxy
of cameras blitzing, you open
your drained face. You cannot hear
the verdict through *a sound
as great as sheer silence.*
Your mouth echoes the vast
structure, sends a mute cry
modulating as it scales
the steep sides of night.
Below pilings, tectonic plates
resound unheard; above,
a chaos of doves; through the void
a satellite steals your visage
for all to scrutinize beyond
the cantilevered air.

Consolation on Pipeline

Sometimes all you want to do is lean
your tired frame against the last post
still upright in the charred settlement
of your life, only the wood is mottled
red with embers and scraps of flame twist
at your feet. Hope zigzags off
to the bruised horizon
like it had been constructed
only to offer perspective.
Face and hands blistered, you toss a pail of water
at a pillar of fire where the market once stood.
The whole world has come
to fill cans in an expanding pool dark
with rainbows. The sky ripples;
a lone heron flies round and round, lost in black clouds.
A truck blazes like a sacred sign.
An acetylene torch rests hidden
in the crotch of the only remaining tree.
Someone viewing from a balcony
of a high-rise on the skyline might have pity
as you slowly dip your hands
in a half-empty basin to wash
the mask of soot from your face.

Particle Accelerator Metaphysics

To hunt for God you have to go underground.
Where once features were found
in the face of a mountain
you now tunnel deep
below thrust fault and crystalline
basement rock, schist and molasse,
to capture the possibility
of a particle less
than a billionth of a millimeter
with a twenty-seven kilometer snare.
Through miles of tunnel,
over catwalks and passing a thousand
cylindrical super-cooled magnets,
amid a million blinking sensors,
while atoms accelerate and collide
invisibly, you wander as if
there were no such thing as oblivion.

Resisting Nostalgia at Hydroelectric Dam

The world submerged
emerges magnified.
You expected
turbulence, not this
surface so still
you can see all
the way to bottom.
From the intake tower
you look down
on streets you once walked
with people you once said you knew
and who said they knew you,
past houses you entered and left
and filled with words and emptied of words.
Curtains still wave out windows
though slowly, so slowly.
It's like you could descend
and pluck a glinting soup can
from the supermarket shelf
or shoot hoops on the playground
or make love by the ghost
river's bank beneath the willow
preserved in cold deep.
The dam contains enough
concrete to bury the whole town
twice over, an improvement on
this structure of forgetting.

The Yam Complex
(Between Time and History)

The Apartment

Returning to a city that held me

For years (but that was years ago),

Even the sky's askew,

Towers for horizon.

Hills now terraced down to the bay

Resemble no contour

Of memory or dream.

Like living an allegory

Missing a deeper half.

One building I recognize,

Stucco now scorched the color of yams,

But the same mushroom cloud

Of bougainvillea rises up

The entire five stories of fire

Escape. A stranger probably

More innocent than I was.

Then occupies the apartment.

Of all that is lost

I remember secondhand

Green-plaid loveseats in front

Of a sealed-off fireplace,

Parrot vases decorating

The narrow mantelpiece,

Eternal fragrance

Of ocean on air, on skin,

The urge to fly over waves.

In the middle stood a pine table

Where I shared plain meals

And studied what was forbidden

And what meant everything

Then. Nothing more

Remembered except the sun

Filtered through vines of magenta

As it moves over a shoulder,

A belly, a hip too beautiful

To reassemble here, now.

But the view! Past the flowers,

A bridge piercing fog, piercing and then

Disappearing. That has remained

Unchanged, as if I had not

Crossed its improbable span

Without destination then.

The Complex

The opposite of labyrinth this

Block upon block of towers

That still after decades I have yet

To call home, a place where I insist

Fate has dropped me without wings.

Here I am miniature yet more

Than public, can never get lost or lose

Myself on the treeless ellipse

Between freeway and cathedral.

Returning from another

Mandatory opportunity

I cross a dusty soccer pitch

Where young men will do anything

For money to buy uniforms.

They sprint and attack with all

The flaws of ancient heroes.

Myth swallows me like

The sea an injured ship.

Millennia pass and then

The elevator simply opens

To aroma of steaming yams,

Sweet thread of memory

Of a country far from here,

Of a country no longer there,

A shimmering country where

A hypnotic bull raises his head

At the scent of a distant oasis

Or storm beyond the maze of sand.

The Compound

The world is contained

Within a compass of runways,

A control tower anchoring the sky,

Contrails indicating possibility

If not promise, if not place.

The compound and surrounding

Plots of yams I've displaced

From memory would fit

Into a single terminal.

Once gods flew.

Now aircraft shatter

Time and latitude

So complete I cannot tell

The story of a world torn open

To the exhausted

Skies beyond.

Island

A Submarine Heaven

Crossing an island accidental
as any land, a trail of crushed shells
underfoot, you come across a skull,
porous, propped in a rock wall,
and guess it belongs to pelican,
swordfish, maybe pterodactyl.
Even in scenarios of arcing slowly
through a galaxy of effervescence
down shelves, past coral, past blue, past light,
to a submarine heaven,
it's easier to imagine
a human than a dolphin dead.

Beyond the Pane

The frescoed cloister is closed.
No echo of omniscience
escapes to wind or metaphor.
A cottage holds three bowls,
earthen and chipped, on a table
made of planks smoothed by surf.
One holds buttermilk;
another, tomatoes pale as moons;
the third, eggs the color of sand.
On the sill you would place a globe
of ivory roses to echo
the dolphin skull beyond the pane,
and think how sonorous, how bold,
this science of solitude.

One Other on Earth

Through shattered words fallen from the shuttered casino,
past rows of cypress like dolphin silhouettes,
under a gathering hurricane of stars,
the lost turn in iron currents,
knowing too late *the great fortune*
of he who can call even one other on earth his own.

Lapidary

Desert at the Heart

As grains of sand strike
your cheek, nick your iris,
words become so small,
unable to contain
what it might mean
for the noonday sun to empty
like an hourglass onto
the carefully articulated
terraces and blunt avenues
of the city of what you loved,
turning it to desert at the heart
of a deep forest of fir
necklaced by reservoirs
cool as jade.

Whirlpool of Our Design

If from the whetstone of legend
a single swallow would scissor
kamikaze straight for the great
whirlpool of our design,
cutting the hydro-turbine,
killing the load through the grid,
blackening the dragon
megalopolis that stretches
down the seaboard, would we
desire the life to come?
And if then, from the starless night,
the moon rose black as pearl,
would a nocturne also rise,
improvisational,
ushering in a paragon republic?

Each Lagoon a Shimmering

Hot wind in winter streams like news crawl
across pine latitudes, through sulfur clouds.
As further warning we could televise
an aerial view of a tropical atoll,
intricate cameos scattered
on the scalloped breast of ocean.
In whorls of coral and wave we might read
tragic profiles, tableaux of greater love
than we will ever live, shorthand epics
of great cities scorched to shadow,
and each lagoon a shimmering lacuna.

Cameos

Lucia
(portrait from Donizetti's *Lucia di Lammermoor*)

on a lonely path by vast ruins of a tower,
through clouds of terror and dim moon, come madness and
love filled with peril, a wedding of deathly pallor, a
great sacrifice for a family's madness love peril *good, but one overpowered by*
sadness, freezes, burns, for this sacrifice blood spirit *fatal love, where threshold and*
nuptial bed are covered with tragedy phantom forgive *blood, as if a spirit*
of hell, and no night can conceal the tragedy, the
clutched blade, the phantom, the lost reason, this unhappy house,
for now the universe is a wasteland, so to die,
to die, o beautiful loving spirit, forgive such a crime

madness love peril
sacrifice blood spirit
   tragedy phantom forgive

Mimi
(portrait from Puccini's *La Bohème*)

love's a stove that squanders fuel, it's freezing out, though
cafes are bright, singing, without rent comes only poetry without
inspiration in a garret, until pale and trembling, a tiny
hand frozen and two lovely singing inspiration poems *eyes steal all possessions, and*
sewing silk roses and lilies roses love passion *that speak of love such*
as only poets know, poems frail angel sleeping *are flowing, but love born*
of passion ends in despair, for it's cold, and growing
weaker, coughing, frail being, all is over, the pen is
useless, no strength to climb the stairs, a muff for
poor frozen hands, sleeping now, hands warmer, an angel, sleeping

singing inspiration poems
roses love passion
frail angel sleeping

Floria
(portrait from Puccini's *Tosca*)

in a chapel, what eyes can equal those dark fiery
eyes, and for the occasion a new cantata, so glitter,
fairest creature, for a handsome traitor, a torture chamber, hands
and feet bound, a ring chapel fiery torture *of iron with spikes, though*
liberty rises victorious, and living liberty art love *for art, for love, and*
never harming a living creature, prayers ascend god *prayers ascend, why lord, for*
then such glowing beauty stabs, the kiss, the blow struck
by a woman, die, die, but the world of love
is murdered anyway, all that is noble and fine hurls
from a parapet into space, in the sight of god

chapel fiery torture
        liberty art love
    prayers ascend god

Norma
(portrait from Bellini's *Norma*)

o moon, hasten, rise among sacred oaks, inspire, prophesy, with
starlight in a troubled sky, engulf the earth in the
sweet peace love gives, lost with seditious voices, while knowing
the source of eternal tears, moon oaks prophesy *and there walking alone, weeping,*
praying, speak out in sublime peace love wrath *tones, for such hopes die*
amid war chants, with pleas sublime forgive tears *appease wrath, the heart betrayed,*
the heart lost, see in this hour what a heart
it was, and with remorse love is reborn, a madder,
more desperate love, now ascend the pyre, there beyond, purer,
holier, begins eternal love, break forth, at last, o tears

moon oaks prophesy
        peace love wrath
sublime forgive tears

Aïda
(portrait from Verdi's *Aïda*)

colonnades, armies, secret love and slavery, war, war, war, return
victorious, sweet joy, cruel anguish, trumpeters, chariots, avenging warrior, prisoners
stretched in the dust, if love of country be a
crime, and from a temple love slavery war *on a starlit night, flee*
to a new country, virgin rapture anguish country *forests, limitless desert, stars will*
shine with clearer light, flee flee tomb eternal *this land of sorrow, love*
shall guide, but then betrayed, dishonored, see now alive in
a tomb in darkness, a phantom, a human form appears,
to die for love, hymn of death, o earth, farewell,
fly to the light of eternal day, peace, peace, peace

love slavery war
rapture anguish country
flee tomb eternal

Cio-Cio San
(portrait from Puccini's *Madama Butterfly*)

over fathomless ocean to harbor where walls come and go,
and everywhere the hue of tea, there a flower hardly
opened, a mirror, a fan, a jar of carmine, dear
almond eyes, a bride robed harbor flower bride in white for night of
rapture, stars unending, blindly loving, rapture sail loving three years gone, a sail
appears, shake the cherry tree abandoned spring knife till every flower flutters down,
though with a scarlet poppy the world is plunged in
gloom, humiliation, and now abandoned, too much light shines outside,
too much laughing spring, now one last look at azure
eyes, go play, play, the knife falling to the ground

harbor flower bride
rapture sail loving
abandoned spring knife

Violetta
(portrait from Verdi's *La Traviata*)

in a mirrored drawing room, raise a glass, burn up
life, though fainting and so pale, how strange to love
with a spirit full of doubt and sick with fever,
but it is love, then only burn spirit fever *to be sacrificed, so*
great a sacrifice, so bitter, love sacrifice farewell *but true until the end,*
so now farewell, smile on noble pain joy *this wayward creature, life is*
misery, it was for love to die so young, after
so much sorrow, all a vain dream, tears of anguish
out of faith and devotion, come close, noble heart, weep,
now join the spirits, the pain has gone, what joy

burn spirit fever
love sacrifice farewell
noble pain joy

visions

eye altar

from oceans of solitude we come
(leaving circumference)

from rooms of words we go
(leaving circumstance)

whenever he appears

up to the altar of his eye
we roll like waves

of light and fall
into his abyss

where image gets exacted
from illusion

where shades
turn spectral

at the eye altar
we are converted

into electricity
snake-dancing

along synapses
to the brain

into cinema remote
from emotion pictures

at the eye altar
we are translated

into thought and vision and
when he leaves we are left

without feature and blind
projecting a sequel

with only the dim slug line
he puts the virtue back in virtual

baroque oculus

disillusioned by this trompe-l'oeil world
we rise like incense past gilt-framed oils
of staked and manacled saints unclad

like crack spiritualists we levitate domeward
into turbulent doomsday and beyond
to infinity constrained by cherubim

up through the oculus we progress to pure
air amid a vortex of pigeons
the sun blowtorching all below to glare

far above the fractured blare of traffic
we rhyme with the pinioned ones
spiraling up artless blue dominion

façade vista

scaling the monumental façade
in search of a fragment of awe
we mime echoes of epic

as toeholds in marble flake off
as handholds crumble dorically

we look for guidance beyond
figures frozen in a frieze

echo epic
beyond the attic

that we may find strength
to surmount impediments
to summit the pediment

grant us vista
that the world may fall
in the ad hoc order of chaos
before us

allow us
freefall
let us fall
and echo

epic to the imprecise end
of a bungee cord

mannahatta

sometimes thoughts echo like the skyline in the harbor . . .

echo 9

oblivious to glances
off the unremitting
diamonds in the window   he leans toward
his own image on the surface
          oblivious to glances
of the reflections
of men he heads westward
to the-river-that-flows-both-ways
never hearing an echo
ancient and clear
of a lenape warrior
going splash
through his own
faceted reflection
becoming the moon

Turning away from the jewelry-store display, he finds a man staring at him—the usual wanting— and, as now, following him down to the Hudson.

here   far from the long acre
of id   the electrified
and digitized screens displaying bodies
of stars in colossal format
dissipate into acid night-
mist   they become abstract
as silent fireworks
          here   away
from the crowd   words
of the two men echo in a twisted naked
canopy of sycamore colored
by what is distant
and by the undiscovered
forge layers of paving below
that once blasted
in this place   in this very air

He listens for something metaphysical beneath his
words—the truth he craves—and does not want
to hear his breath tighten with desire, so glances
toward the stone lions.

in the silence that loiters above
a river of taxis   full of room-service
pulled pork and a mediocre vintage
pulling on cigarettes
the two lie head-to-toe
soldier-style on a bedspread
emblazoned with loss
looking onto the city so lit
even arcturus is invisible
though nevertheless bleeding
infrared through every window
of the graven limestone and steel
skyline   through every fractal
of basalt shoreline
through the narrow confines
of this light year

---

*He's been thinking about this for hours as he
stares toward the Park, thinking how he wants
to beat off without being touched, with him just
watching.*

only one of them notes
as they exit the subway
rattus norvegicus sipping the dark
iridescent puddle between tracks
or in the museum
the lacy angel skeleton
archaeopteryx lithographica
faux lizard   faux bird
pressed into limestone or
atrax robustus
funnel-web spider spinning
silk out so slow and so like this
homo-sapien's slow
string of saliva stretching
and attaching to the hollow
at the base of the other's cock last night

He knows he shouldn't be wasting his days like this, acting as though they have a future outside of allegory.

in a crowd one of them looks down
at his own crotch   adjusts
his equipment as if
to make sure it is still
there or maybe just to stop
that zero sensation
of being in a place
unremembered   here
where the post road once ran
by a brook that once ran
as it passed into marsh that once was
and the elm   the elm   almost
a memory   and nearby
wolf tracks   their faint trace
petrified many strata below
                        and then a memory
                        of moonlight
like this   or maybe just a feeling
of collective desolation
that's all   as he shifts
his vitals again

_____

Lost in the space between them like he's always
been, only worse, like Washington Square is
the abyss.

echo 112

a warm cello bows
deeply   horsehair flies
catgut snaps   but the note
that note   the same once heard
by a rowdy b'hoy
stilling his rowboat
in the river just to catch
traces of the sublime
(long lost even then)
escaping the concert hall
into the hot night

For once, blessedly, he forgets them, the two
of them. They disappear into the audience;
the audience disappears.

two a.m. and a hand made
for sunlit orchards reaches high
among rows of cool amber and green
and clear bottles backlit
      luminous
she serves them
touching the cheek of the one
offering cascades of something
like laughter   something
like indifference to the other
lost as any suitor
in the maze of apple trees
that long ago grew on this plot

―――――――――――――――――――――

Their friendship had taken a turn in
Tribeca only one of them was aware of.

across from the vestigial
firehouse on a fire escape
the one dons a fire-engine
red feather boa before proceeding
to perch on the torso
of the other
as the woman
and dawn advance
all at once   the intricacies
of whispers get lost in the growl
of garbage trucks   the desired effect
   the effect of desire
and then the one posing
as carrion rises
and retreats down flights
to where mules once towed barges   hailing
the lone yellow cab as a hawk-owl
swoops from the cornice
causing a firestorm
of pigeons on the china sky

From this night on the outskirts of Chinatown,
he accepts coming days of grief and jealousy.

echo 228

green eyes made greener still
by gray sky and still grayer
façades make the one
crossing with the crowd seem more
like he is arriving
like the arrival
of glory-hero or
sacrifice   precision
bruises shine along his muscled throat
a white cloud rising from
a manhole swallows him
as he greets the other
with a reinvented gesture
of love and moves him
to the lit lobby and then
into the dark movie house

---

*How could he have known that what he would
want most—right there in front of the Angelika—
now that he finally had the chance to see him
again, was to meet the one whose teeth had
marked his throat, to offer her goodwill and
hope for all happiness?*

Stars

What the Stars Will Bring

When there's nothing left
Consider the stars fading overhead,
A stranger passing on the bridge,
Random words overheard.
Forget astrology.
Take the stars literally,
The bridge as metaphor,
The stranger as familiar.
Take metaphor as metaphor.
Carry the stranger over
To Orion at zenith,
To a noir hero
In the shadows of the pier.
Every step desire.
Every step disaster.
It isn't written in the stars.
It is written in a constellation
Of syllables collapsing
Along your synapses
Into electric silence.

What Morning Will Bring

On the span between night and day,
Between embankment lined by sycamore
And embankment scattered with asters,
You understand your glance
Amounts to nothing, an asterisk
On a stranger's unconscious.
The world's worst flaneur,
You regret the extravagant
Vagrancy your life's become,
The exorbitant desire to orbit
Among stars and crowds.
Somewhere ecstasy is simpler:
The sun coming on like a pop song,
Waking not knowing your own tattoos,
This ex-stranger becoming strange again.

elements of a boy

his small self constant / variable

unlatched from familiar
shadows on sand

he wades into kaleidoscope
blue green gray ~

scooping stones from the flux
he calculates

every pebble's coast
every pebble's tide

horizon to horizon
zone to zone ~

water streams through his fingers
silver threads

in the robe of probability
folding and unfolding

around his small self constant
variable ~ the solution

gets lost in the echo
of a voice forgotten

in the echo of a name lost
in the ocean's volume

in the shadow
running toward him ~

private pantheon

past the last cul-de-sac
he hollows out
from the clay bank
a private pantheon

he creates each god
in his own image
stolen from the river
and seals them in

without signet
without regret

top's down

wind evidence of air and abstract as ecstasy flooding him standing
        on the backseat arms encircling the neck of the father exceeding all

in the shape of a shield

dog-
shadow
rising wolf-

like in light
from a birthday
cake; six

candles;
terror of making
a wish

as the honey-
comb of self fills
reluctantly

with air; slate clouds
fall through sun;
the dog orbits

its own body
just once;
wind through pane

creates minute
hurricanes crisscrossing
the room;

candles flare
like a forest on fire;
exhaling

at last;
the sun revives;
the yard ignites;

maple shade flickers
over family
faces masked

by candlelight;
cake-knife blazes
like a sword;

ice-blue wax rains
across the tundra
of sugar; a scroll

of smoke unrolls
through space
and he reads

triumph or suffer
as the dog sinks back
into the corner,

curling down
in the shape
of a shield

Proceeding from Emotion

Apparently Only Writing

We are soldiers
with the sun and the sand
in our eyes.

We proclaim our tears
are not real
but reflex. We see them

from the outside only,
gleaming globes
reflecting the world

as they balance
on the red rim
of a mother's eye,

like in an oil painting.
We admire detail
and never see

those are the eyelets
of our own boots glinting
as we fall,

never see that she is
holding a book
in her lap

and writing:

Apparently
only writing,

war, and tears
distinguish us
from the animals.

We Would Compose Ourselves

If we knew the world we'd weep
and then say we were crying
for no apparent reason.
We'd push our mother
standing there, freighted
with sorrow, into the revolution
of random thought called memory.
We would assemble
a landscape around her,
evaporating all particulars
from her history:
The news arrived,
just like you'd think,
in pressed uniform,
and the sun continued to shine
regardless of desire,
ditto the freeway whirring behind the house,
ditto the fucking soundtrack
of my life blaring from the kitchen dock.

Our Own News

We're each on our own
endless mail route in this
circular world where nothing
essential is ever delivered:
no lock of hair,
no locket with portrait
in vivid enamel,
no announcements
of birth or death
in ink and words both
carefully chosen,
no thorny love letter
in erratic hand,
no blackmail note
in precise cursive,
no thought colored by or
proceeding from emotion.
We carry on, and they
don't let us know
we've gotten our own news
until we are finished:
If you beat a dog hard enough
it will produce tears.

seeing

night-blooming cereus

always we see only
within limits: a cone

of light pushing through
desert night: galaxies

of insects revealed and
interrupted: in the rearview

maybe saturn and the moon
eclipsed by a penumbra of bats:

if the *ghost scent*
(as the pima know it)

could be noticed at eighty m.p.h.
would we then turn

our helmeted heads to see
the sidereal silhouette

if not the flower itself in bloom
just this one night of the year

in just this one place:

junked

junked by the invisible world
concentrate on aphids

           swarming slo-mo on the underside
           of maroon velvet coleus leaves

on a single cicada perched on a porch rail
thrumming its armored abdomen

           on how a dog drinks backwards
           pulling water under tongue

on altitude glowing
from the altimeter in a cockpit

           on gravity as something concrete
           pulling at a cylinder of clay

as it spins on a wheel and starts
wobbling in widening parabolas

           on the clear hemisphere
           of a planetarium containing the chaos of space

junked by the visible world
you start desiring ecstatic acid

           scars on a stone anterior
           to the limits of the lithograph

the sound of cicadas vibrating out
from the crown of a sycamore

           the celestial view
           of earth offered by in-flight booze

stars at noon sun at night
a solar eclipse in a pail of water

        a shadow of the lost
        ivory bill sweeping across a forest floor

notes of a fugue hollowing out
spandrels and vaults of air

        spray of stars shot over waves
        over a body asleep beneath a window

      and you read *internal* as *infernal*
      external as *eternal*
      in the pages of a familiar book

Bear Rock

Two rocks   similar and not
similar   dissimilar and not

dissimilar   the space between
articulated   by pebbles

raked in silence
                  (soft scratching of tines)

into patterns of
curves interlocking curves

A valley between two mountains
articulated by   pines and mist

rising silent
            (soft rustling of needles)

in undulating patterns   broken
by the trajectory   of a bear

A person enters a garden   kneels at the edge
of raked pebbles   A bear comes down

from the mountains   enters a garden
making an arc of tracks   across raked patterns

A person leaves a garden
goes to the mountains   following

a marked trail
A bear and a rock   a bear

in the shape of a rock   a rock
in the shape of a bear   A person

mistakes a rock for a bear   a person
almost never mistakes a bear for a rock

at any distance
A bear never mistakes   a rock or

a person for anything ever
In the dark   in a cave

in a mountain   a bear rakes
its claws down the wall

On a cave wall   lit
                              (by tallow in a hollowed rock)

a person paints a bear
barehanded   using a pattern

of claw marks to represent
fur   The flame

animates the bear
the bear becomes anima

five appearances

you appear last in a pillar of dust
the surrounding air complicated
by anachronism
by glint of shield and spear
you are sacrifice without cipher

last meaning previous

you appear last in a helix of snow
intricate geometries ticking
without synchrony
against bronze oak leaves
against nylon parka
ticking in absence of teleology

last meaning remaining

you appear last under arcs of water
light hammering your blurred torso
your voice resounding with the falling
water off shale
and the words
the word
then what did you say

last meaning continue

you appear last against a sky
febrile and full of birds
convolutions of grackles
not canada geese in orderly v's
there is grace and there is grace

last meaning final

you appear last at night
a spume of stars
echoing your body
a chevron of jade swinging
from a leather cord at your throat
keeps time with hermetic cantos
for this last supplicant
mouth open like fish to lure

last meaning survive

bound

no escaping this net of words

sound woven to sound so

                    speak low as we fall into this net

                    listen far as we sway

in this hammock anchored

by white pines conspiring

                    in the breeze above

                    elliptical river tones

no escaping this net of light

ray knotted to ray to

eagle-shadow unbroken

as it sweeps over our bodies

and over random weave

of rust needles below

to eagle seen broken through

dust-green needles above

no escaping this net of skin

cell knit to cell to cell

        however close we press

        in the cooling atmosphere

cooling from blue to red

at last bleeding plum to

        black as boats dredge the bed

        for a child lost upstream

no escaping this net of stars

galaxy twisted and tied

into patterns of astronomical

creatures from a far archipelago

scorpion crab fish circling fish

centaur with bow drawn back

no escaping this net of thought

neuron woven to neuron

invisible lines

of longitude and latitude

        a crossword a lobster trap

        a trellis of morning glory

a map of manhattan

a loose-woven canopy

        pitched in turbulent desert

        air resounding with *aleph*

(that syllable called to recall a far

faceless god) crosshatching

        suddenly becoming a portrait

        with the artist's final strokes

or your fingers woven into mine

this single gesture of closing

        the openwork holding

        nebulous patterns beyond

COLOPHON

darkacre was designed at Coffee House Press, in the historic
Grain Belt Brewery's Bottling House near downtown Minneapolis.
The text is set in Garamond.

FUNDER ACKNOWLEDGMENTS

Publication of this book was made possible in part, as a result of a grant from the National Endowment for the Arts, a federal agency, because a great nation deserves great art. Coffee House Press receives major operating support from the Bush Foundation, the McKnight Foundation, from Target, and from the Minnesota State Arts Board, through an appropriation from the Minnesota State Legislature and from the National Endowment for the Arts. Coffee House also receives support from: three anonymous donors; Abraham Associates; the Elmer L. and Eleanor J. Andersen Foundation; Allan Appel; Around Town Literary Media Guides; Bill Berkson; the James L. and Nancy J. Bildner Foundation; the Patrick and Aimee Butler Family Foundation; the Buuck Family Foundation; Dorsey & Whitney, LLP; Fredrikson & Byron, P.A.; Jennifer Haugh; Anselm Hollo and Jane Dalrymple-Hollo; Jeffrey Hom; Stephen and Isabel Keating; Robert and Margaret Kinney; the Kenneth Koch Literary Estate; Allan & Cinda Kornblum; the Lenfestey Family Foundation; Ethan J. Litman; Mary McDermid; Rebecca Rand; Debby Reynolds; Schwegman, Lundberg, Woessner, P.A.; Charles Steffey and Suzannah Martin; John Sjoberg; Jeffrey Sugerman; Stu Wilson and Mel Barker; the Archie D. & Bertha H. Walker Foundation; the Woessner Freeman Family Foundation in memory of David Hilton; and many other generous individual donors.

This activity is made possible
in part by a grant from the
Minnesota State Arts Board,
through an appropriation by the
Minnesota State Legislature
and a grant from the National
Endowment for the Arts.

NATIONAL
ENDOWMENT
FOR THE ARTS

MINNESOTA
STATE ARTS BOARD

TARGET.

To you and our many readers across the country,
we send our thanks for your continuing support.

Good books are brewing at www.coffeehousepress.org